How to Master Landscape Painting in 24 Hours! A Seven-Step Guide for Oil Painting the Landscape Today

By: Jeremiah Jolliff

How to Master Landscape Painting in 24 Hours! A
seven-Step Guide for Oil Painting the Landscape Today
Jeremiah Jolliff
www.ArtworkByJJ.com

Jeremiah Jolliff is a fine artist from Camden Ohio in the United States.

Before going on his own Jeremiah had a career in the United States Air Force and the United States Antarctic Program as the Senior Meteorologist at Amundsen-Scott South Pole Station. Today, Jeremiah works with artists and entrepreneurs from around the world helping them to successfully create, publish and promote their work.

Jeremiah's primary focus is helping artists and entrepreneurs strategically position themselves. Achieving rapid growth of business by attracting ideal clients and charging higher fees.

This book is dedicated to my family for believing in me, my friends for their tolerance, and capitalism for making it all possible.

Thank you for a lifetime of support and encouragement.

"I dream my painting and I paint my dream."
-Vincent Van Gogh

"However one's mind may be elevated, and kept as to what is excellent, by the works of the Great Masters, – still Nature is the fountain's head, the source form whence all originality must spring."
-John Constable

"All you need to paint is a few tools, a little instruction, and a vision in your mind."
-Bob Ross

"Builders and warriors, strengthen the steps. Reader, if you have not grasped — read again, after a while. The predestined is not accidental; the leaves fall in their time. And winter is but the harbinger of spring. All is revealed; all is attainable."
-Nicholas Roerich

"The great secret of Freemasonry is that there is no secret at all."
-Benjamin Franklin

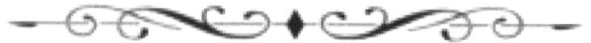

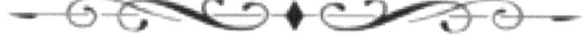

Introduction

I would like to discuss how this book came about. The development of this book came about by extensive note taking in the field. I wrote this book to help other landscape painters gain traction and become fluent in the art of landscape painting quickly.

This book is organized into seven-steps and expedites the reader out of the studio and into the field as quickly as possible. The first step is to gather materials and then move seamlessly into the next steps. The last part of the book is a short exercise where the artist can practice what they learned in the studio before stepping outside. Completing the short exercise builds confidence and helps the artist become accustomed to the process.

The reader will be relieved that this seven-step guide is easy to follow and gives the artist the tools to produce artwork efficiently. The purpose of this book is to save the artist time and give them direct advice without the fluff.

The journey to writing this book has been long and enjoyable. Modern art has pretty much wiped out the knowledge of the craft of painting. I read many old books on how the impressionists were able to produce such high forms of art with limited materials. The only problem is that those books are very smart and often hard to decipher owing to the author's high intellect and more informed language.

Also, formatting this book as an ebook was quite a challenge. If there are formatting mistakes, my fault...

If you want free tips and would like to contact me, go to my website now and opt-in: http://www.artworkbyjj.com/

All of my artwork is available for sale as originals and prints, along with painting tutorials, recommended products, and more.

My Website: http://www.artworkbyjj.com/

https://www.facebook.com/ARTWORKBYJEREMIAHJOLLIFF

Blog: https://jjolliffblog.wordpress.com/

Twitter: https://twitter.com/jeremiahjollif

Youtube:
https://www.youtube.com/channel/UCsauBxqWjjow6bCKl7DgRHA

LinkedIn: https://www.linkedin.com/in/jeremiahjolliff

Google+:
https://plus.google.com/u/0/+JeremiahJolliffartwork/posts/p/pub

Instagram: https://instagram.com/jeremiah_jolliff/

Pinterest: https://www.pinterest.com/jeremiahjolliff/

10

Chapter 1 Step 1 - How to Prepare Materials

Materials

It is overwhelming to figure out what to purchase for landscape painting. Everyone's advice is different. Art suppliers market all kinds of materials that are unnecessary. The following is *the* definitive list of supplies required. In this chapter, I will give the complete list of items that are necessary for a successful day landscape painting. I will list the items and then give short descriptions. After the descriptions, I will describe how to prepare the materials before going into the field. Organization is a necessity. Here is a list to make things easy.

Materials list:

Lightweight Tripod

Portable Easel / pochade Box

8" x 10" canvas boards

#18 pure red sable flat Brush (1)

#4 Hog Bristle Filbert Brush (2)

#3 Hog Bristle Filbert Brush (2)

#2 Hog Bristle Filbert Brush (2)

Palette Knife

Palette

Paper Towels

A re-sealable container for medium

Turpentine

Linseed Oil

Copal Medium

Neutral colored shirt to wear while painting

A hat

A Good Backpack

Vine Charcoal & knead-able erasers

Viewfinder

Titanium White

Cadmium Lemon

Cadmium Yellow Medium

Cadmium Orange

Cadmium Red

Indian Red

Alizarin Crimson

Cobalt Blue

Ivory Black

Yellow Ochre

Raw Sienna

Burnt Sienna

Sap Green

Viridian

Empty Aluminum Paint Tubes

Descriptions of Materials

Lightweight Tripod- It is important to have a very lightweight aluminum tripod. Often times it is necessary to walk vast distances. A normal tripod used for photography should work just fine.

Portable Easel / Pochade Box- a portable easel usually has a tripod that is built in. As a result, if one has a portable easel, then the tripod is not necessary. However, if one has a pochade box, then a tripod is necessary. A pochade box usually has a "screw in" attachment that will easily attach to an aluminum tripod just like camera. I prefer to work with Pochade Box and aluminum tripod because it is easier to carry.

8" x 10" canvas boards- an 8" x 10" canvas board may seem small but it is easier to manage. When painting outdoors, time is of the essence. For that reason, it is a good idea to start small. Small paintings can be completed faster than large paintings. Besides, canvas boards are small enough to be stowed away when hiking or traveling to a good location, and are less likely to fly off the easel like a kite during windy conditions.

Brushes- a sable brush is great to use when painting the sky because the bristles are very supple and allow the sky to be painted flat (more on this in chapter 4). In regards to the hog bristle brushes, it is a good idea to have two of each size. Keep one for painting light and the other for painting in dark values. Having two brushes of each size will greatly aid the artist in working efficiently. Two brushes help the artist to work efficiently because there is no need to constantly clean brushes when switching between light and dark values.

Palette Knife- a flexible medium sized palette knife will do the trick. The best are tapered towards the end, are flexible and help the artist to not only mix paint on the palette but scrape out areas upon the canvas.

Palette- a palette made of wood is best. I suggest buying a medium sized palette and coat it several times with linseed oil before using it. As time goes by, the palette will begin to take on a very neutral grey color. Having a good, aged palette helps the artist to determine color more accurately.

Paper towels- bring a whole roll of cheap paper towels into the field. Having a large quantity of paper towels pays dividends because they can be used for things unimaginable.

Resealable Container- I prefer to use a small plastic container with a metal lid. Do not use glass. If glass is used, the artist will regret this because it will undoubtedly break in the field.

Turpentine- a high quality turpentine is a necessity. Do not buy turpenoid or odorless mineral spirits.

Linseed oil- the artists purchase only artist's grade linseed oil.

Copal medium- taken together with a high quality linseed oil makes a great medium for painting whilst outdoors.

Neutral colored shirt- it is a good idea to wear a very neutral, usually earth toned shirt. If the shirt is bright or a lively color, there will be a reflection onto the canvas and the painting will look extremely different once brought indoors.

Vine Charcoal & knead-able erasers- vine charcoal erases easily and knead-able erasures can easily remove charcoal dust.

A Hat- it is a good practice to always have a hat when painting outside because of wind, precipitation and sun. I personally like to wear the same hat and the same shirt, whenever I go out painting. It certainly helps to put one into character!

Backpack- this is a very important and often overlooked aspect of landscape painting. There needs to be a lot of room, a few different compartments for paint and brushes and important stuff like food and water. Having food and water and maybe even another layer of clothing could become essential. One must plan for the unexpected when leaving the comfortable confines of the studio and venturing out into the wilds. Use a dedicated backpack for landscape painting. Keep all your gear together and be at the ready.

Oil Paint- Purchase artist grade color only. Do not purchase student grade color because there is too much filler in student grade oil paint and the tinting strength is greatly reduced thereby. Go ahead and commit to buying the higher quality paint. The pain brought to the pocket book by purchasing materials may act as a catalyst to make one go paint more often.

Empty Paint Tubes- these come in extremely handy for re-tubing paint or creating color in the studio that can be used in the field. A good example would be to create a basic sky blue color that can be adjusted easily once out in the field. Two more such examples of this practice would be to pre-mix a basic tree green and a basic meadow green. For example, I pre-mix a sky blue, a tree green and a meadow green. The recipes for these colors will be given later in this chapter.

Viewfinder- prismacolor makes an excellent adjustable viewfinder. A viewfinder helps the artist make decisions on composition and is a good aid used to draw the landscape onto the canvas board with charcoal.

How to Prepare the Materials

How to prepare the Canvas Panels- At home
in the studio the night before, lay out a bunch of those 8" x 10" canvas panels, turpentine, a big paint brush, palette, paper towels, and last but not least, raw sienna.

Take the raw sienna and put a small pile of it onto the palette.

Next, pour a small quantity of turpentine onto the palette with the raw sienna.

Take a big paintbrush and mix it around on the palette until the consistency is thin & uniform.

Apply the mixture onto the canvas boards & wipe off the

excess with paper towels.

The Raw Sienna should be fairly transparent on the canvas panel boards. The turpentine acts as a dryer for the raw sienna oil paint. These canvas panels will be ready to paint upon in a few hours.

These raw sienna toned canvas boards are excellent to paint upon outdoors. The reason for this is because when a painter paints cool colors onto a warm background, it produces a scintillating sensation. Once the painter experiences that joy first-hand, it is never forgotten.

Most outdoor scenes are very cool in nature: cool blue sky, relaxing greens of the grassy fields, trees laden with atmosphere in the distance. When the painter paints these forms into a raw sienna toned board, the wow factors goes through the stratosphere.

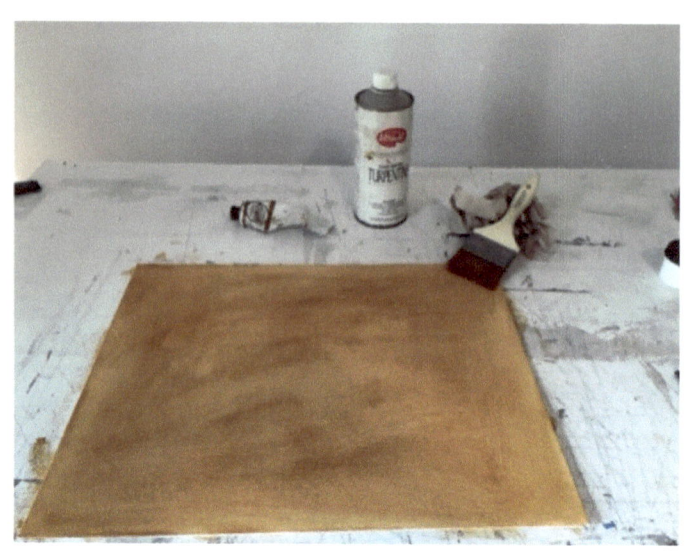

How to prepare Sky Blue, Tree Green, & Meadow Green

How to prepare Sky Blue- For sky blue the mixture is straightforward enough and consists of only four colors: Cobalt Blue, Alizarin Crimson, Burnt sienna, & titanium white.

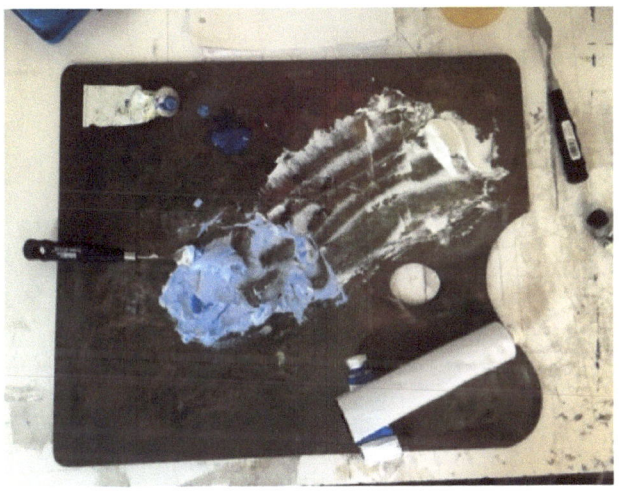

Take a large dollop of cobalt blue along with a heap of white. It should be a mixture of something like 65% titanium white and 35% cobalt blue. Add to this pile a modicum of alizarin crimson and a modicum of the burnt sienna.

Adding a modicum of burnt sienna should gray the mixture down because no matter how perfectly azure blue the sky can appear, there is always a measure of gray in the sky.

Adding a modicum of alizarin crimson is the biggest secret Donald Trump card a painter can wield. There is a certain level of electricity in alizarin crimson and the interaction it has with every color on the palette is a subtle one and is very easily over done. The tinting strength of alizarin crimson is strong; therefore, exercise caution. In other words, use the correct amount.

How to Prepare Tree Green- Tree green is pretty simple to prepare. Simply add these colors together: raw sienna, yellow ochre, burnt sienna and about half and half viridian and sap green.

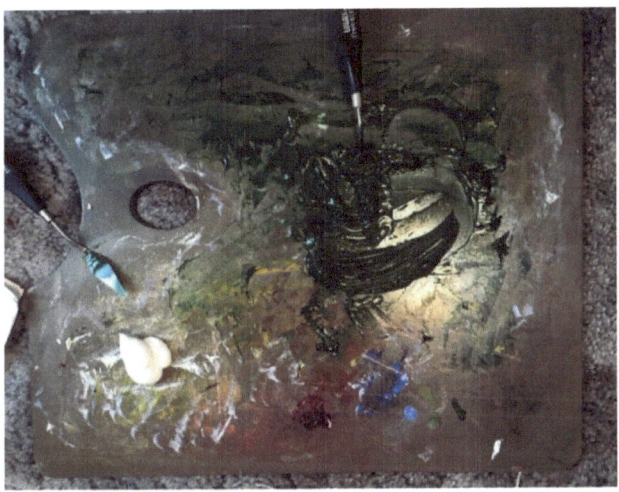

It must be left up to the artist to determine the exact percentages of these component colors to make tree green. If these colors are used and experimented with, the results will be good enough to paint almost any tree or vegetation that has some variation of green in it.

How to Prepare Meadow Green- Meadow green
is almost always much lighter in value than the tree green just
mentioned. Simply take these colors and mix them together
in various percentages: burnt Sienna, sap green, yellow ochre,
& a heap of titanium white.

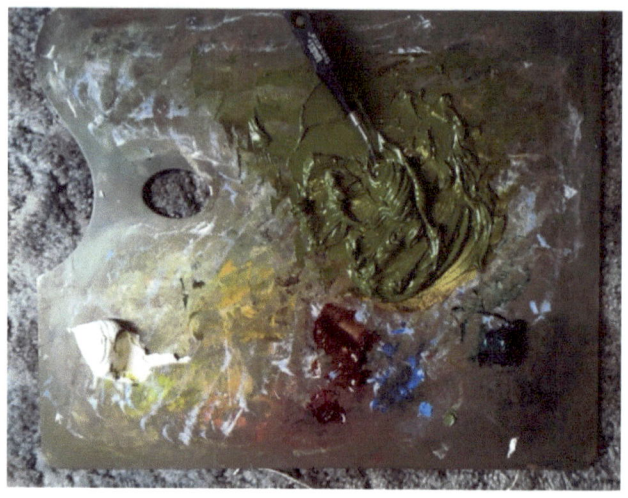

How to Prepare a Basic Tree Trunk Color-

Tree trunks are simply a mixture of cobalt blue and burnt sienna with the addition of a heap of white.

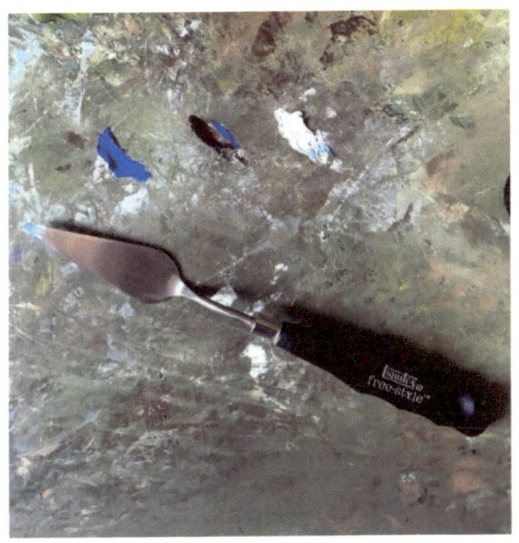

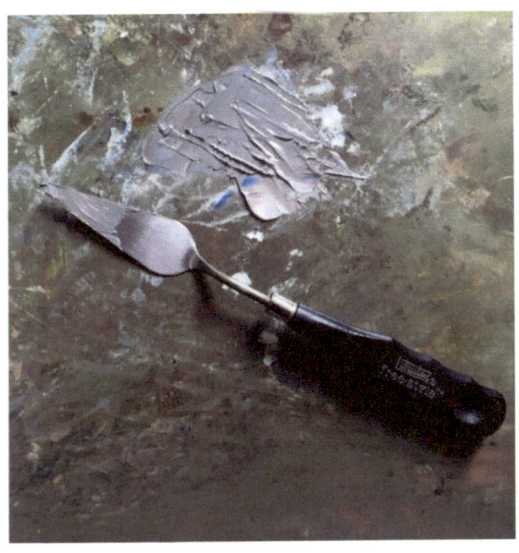

Once one has all these mixtures prepared, it can be somewhat convenient to tube them up in empty aluminum tubes.

How to Prepare the Palette- Lay out the palette in this order from the top row left to right: ivory black, sky blue mixture, cobalt blue, alizarin crimson, Indian red, cadmium red, cadmium orange, cadmium yellow medium, cadmium lemon, heap of titanium white. The second row from left to right consists of: Viridian green, sap green, burnt sienna, raw sienna, yellow ochre. The third row from left to right is: tree green & meadow green.

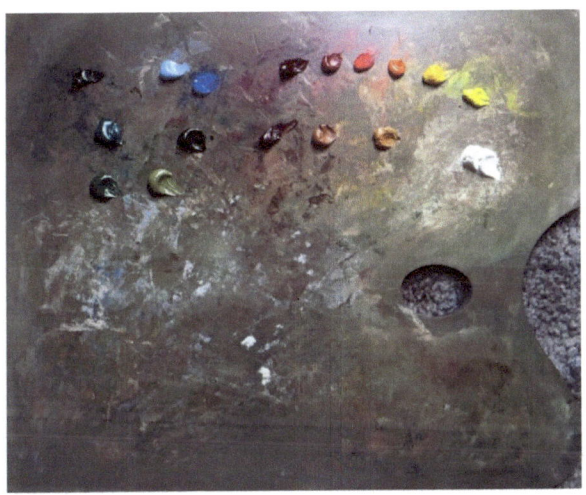

How to prepare the medium- The painting medium is used to thin the paint down enough so that it flows off the brush more easily. Take about 50% linseed oil and 50% copal medium and put them in a small re-sealable container and shake the mixture together. If one adds more Copal Medium the concoction will dry more quickly. If one adds more linseed oil the concoction will dry more slowly.

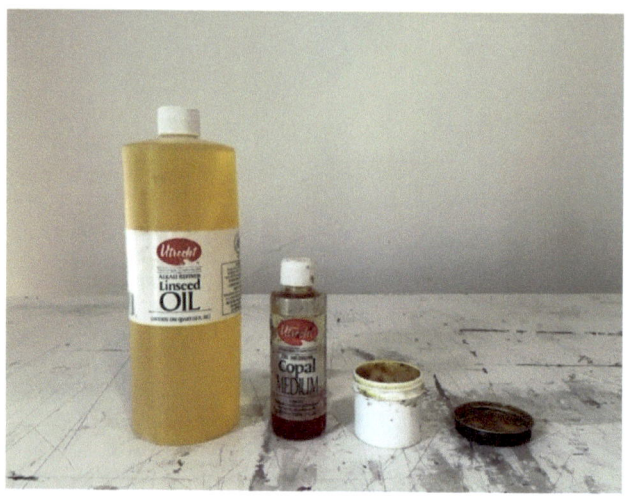

Chapter 2 Step 2 - How to Draw a Landscape

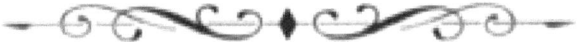

How to Draw a Landscape

Once the artist has determined an excellent area to paint and has everything all set up, take the viewfinder and frame a composition.

The most effective way to draw a landscape is to first draw in the largest lines. The largest or longest line in a landscape painting is the horizon line. Do not place the horizon line exactly in the middle of the canvas board. It is best to place it on one of the thirds. In other words, place the horizon line either 1/3 up or 2/3 up in the composition.

Take a piece of charcoal and make a mark on the each side of the viewfinder where the horizon is located. Use your marks made on the viewfinder and place the same marks on each side of the canvas. Connect the two marks with a line to establish the horizon line and the lay of the land onto the canvas.

29

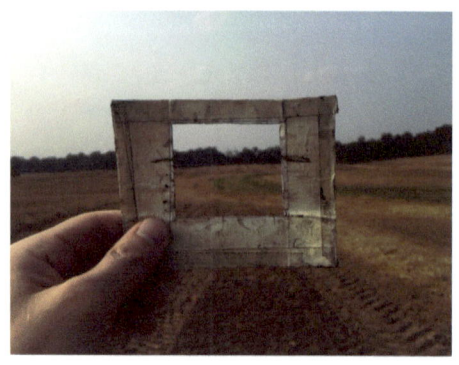

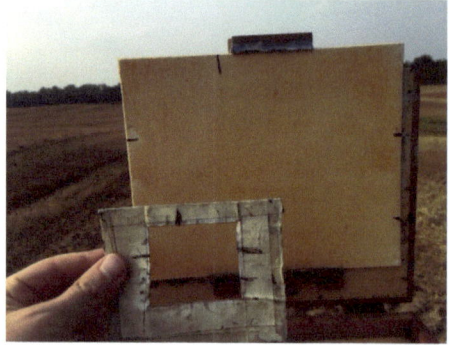

The next largest line in a landscape painting is often a tree, a telephone pole or a building. Use the viewfinder and charcoal once again to make marks on the sides of the viewfinder and then copy these marks onto the canvas. Use these marks as reference points to help draw in the rest composition.

Continue this process by breaking things down— working from establishing the largest line to the smallest line. I always repeat things to myself, when I am landscape painting. For example: "the horizon line is 1/3 up the side of the viewfinder and that big tree starts about 1/3 to the left and that building is about 1/2 as tall as the tree," and so on.

The layout of a landscape painting with charcoal is the most important aspect of the whole operation. During this step, the artist is building the structure on which the adornments of paint are to be applied. Take time during this portion to make it proportional. Enough cannot be said about an artist's integrity at this stage.

If one knows that the line just drawn is out of proportion, the necessary step is to erase it and draw it again. There is only one true line. Stay balanced, stay focused and draw the lines correctly because everything that comes later depends on solid draftsmanship.

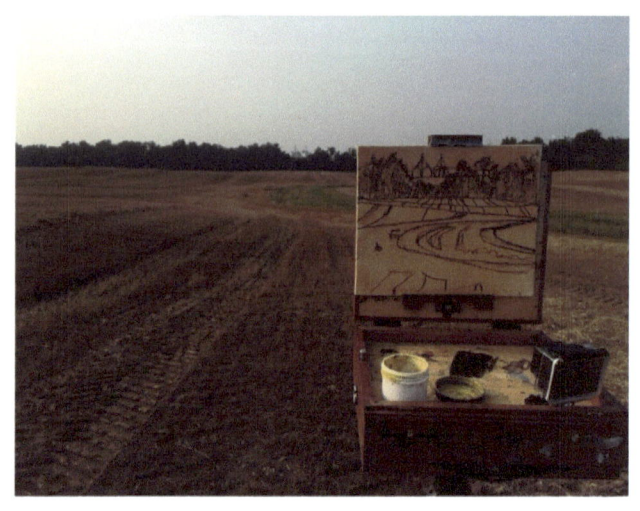

Chapter 3 Step 3 - How to do an Underpainting

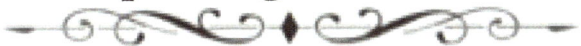

How to do an Underpainting

Once the drawing is well established onto the raw sienna toned canvas board, one can go back and establish the shadow shapes with raw sienna. Simply go over the large shadow shapes with raw sienna thinned with the painting medium of 50% copal & linseed oil. Keep the paint thin, so that there is time for it to dry a bit before painting the next layer.

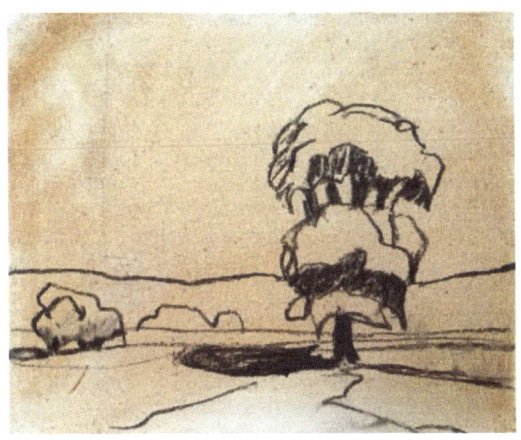

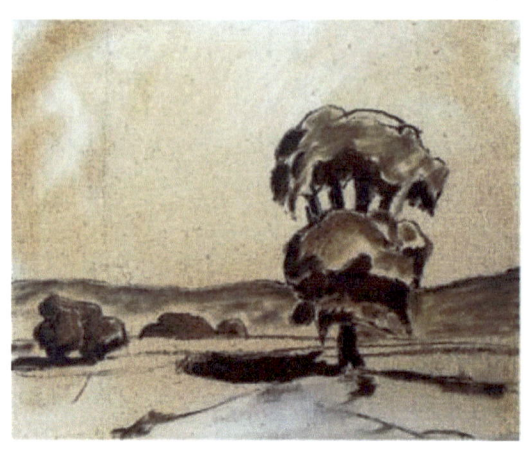

Values relationships in a Landscape are as follows: the sky (lightest value), the flat ground (light half tone), near vertical objects (dark half tone), & vertical objects & their cast shadows (darkest value).

The sky- is almost always the brightest in a Landscape except for when there is snow upon the ground or if a human made structure is painted white, highly reflective, or of similar modern building material.

The flat ground- is a light value because it is perpendicular to the light source and receives the full force of light from the directly from the sky. That black asphalt road isn't black at all!

Near vertical objects- like hill sides absorb less light because their slopes are at obscure angles in regards to the direction of the light source and are therefore darker in value than the flat ground but everything depends on sun angle and distance from the painter.

Vertical objects- like trees and buildings have angles almost parallel to the light rays and usually capture less light unless their limbs or walls are broad side or facing the sun.

Shadows- are usually the darkest nearest the structure from which they were cast. The further away a shadow is from its parent object, the more light diffuses the shadow and the weaker it becomes.

Use the raw sienna to further establish these value relationships and large shadow shapes. For example if there is a huge barn and one side of it is in shadow, paint the whole side of that barn with raw sienna. The medium should dry quick enough so that it can be painted over with a nice purple red color without the raw sienna lifting up from the canvas too much.

Establishing the values using raw sienna helps the overall composition. Areas of shadows, areas of middle value and areas of light must be established. When I am painting my underpainting, I always talk to myself and say: "where is my darkest dark in this composition? Where is my highest value? The shadow on the side of the barn is brighter than the shadow under that bush over there."

As one becomes more experienced, it becomes apparent that there is a lot of dialogue that goes on. "How tall is that barn compared to that tree? How dark is that shadow under that tree when compared to the shadow underneath the roof of this house?"

Another key element of painting an underpainting with raw sienna is that it increases the scintillation of light. Here is an example of what I mean: suppose there is a grassy field and upon this field there is a tree and underneath this tree is a shadow. The other areas of the field are in daylight.

If the painter paints the areas of shadow underneath the tree with raw sienna to its proper dark value, and then applies the cool green shadow colors of the same dark value on the raw sienna, the matching values of cool colors on top of warm colors creates scintillation.

Areas of the grass that are not in the shadow of the tree have a light value green. The light value green needs to be painted over a light value raw sienna. It may even become necessary to take a paper towel dampened with a bit of painting medium and further wipe out the raw sienna under-tone so that the white of the canvas shines through rendering a lighter value.

When painting on top of the underpainting let areas of that raw sienna break through here and there. That adds a nice scintillating effect called broken color.

Here is a quote from Birge Harrison in his book entitled Landscape Painting:

> "Vibration is obtained by means of a cool overtone painted freshly into a warm undertone, care being taken not to mix or blend the two coats and not cover up completely the undertone, rather letting it show through brokenly all over the canvas; the vibration being secured, naturally, by the separate play of warm and cold notes."

Chapter 4 Step 4 - How to Paint the Sky

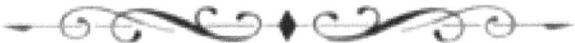

How to Paint the Sky

Birge Harrison advises:

> "Paint a sunny sky in two simple tones, using say, a delicate gray pink for the underlay and a blue green for the overlay, varying the color from the horizon up as it occurs in nature. In the first experiment mix the overlay with extreme care until its value exactly matches the underlay. Then mix another lot of the green blue either slightly darker or slightly lighter than the underlay. Apply these tones each to one-half of the prepared sky, and you will find that the sky painted with the perfectly matched tone will fly away infinitely, and will be bathed in a perfect atmosphere, while the other half of the canvas remain merely paint and canvas - nature deals in broken color everywhere, but she never deals in broken values. The color dances, but the values stay put."

What an esoteric statement to the profane! Once the artist begins to landscape paint in earnest, this statement will make a lot more sense. Until then, I will give some simple advice to paint a simple blue sky.

Take one of the canvas boards toned with raw sienna. Draw a simple horizon line about 1/3 up from the bottom of the canvas board. Take the sky blue mixture and paint it across the top of the canvas board. As one progresses downward towards the horizon line, keep adding more titanium white, a small quantity of alizarin crimson and cadmium orange. Its that easy, when painting on top of a raw sienna toned board.

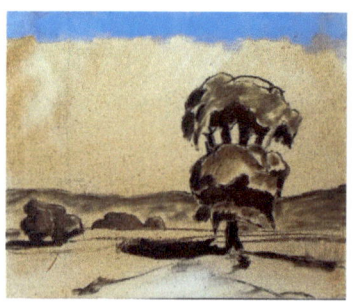

But what if there are clouds in the sky?

Here are some pointers for painting a fair weather day with a few clouds. Use the same instruction above to paint another sky. Next take the sky blue and add some burnt sienna in order to create the shadows that are underneath the clouds. As the clouds recede from the viewer's eye however, the shadows become more blue and lighter in value underneath the clouds and may not require burnt sienna in the mixture.

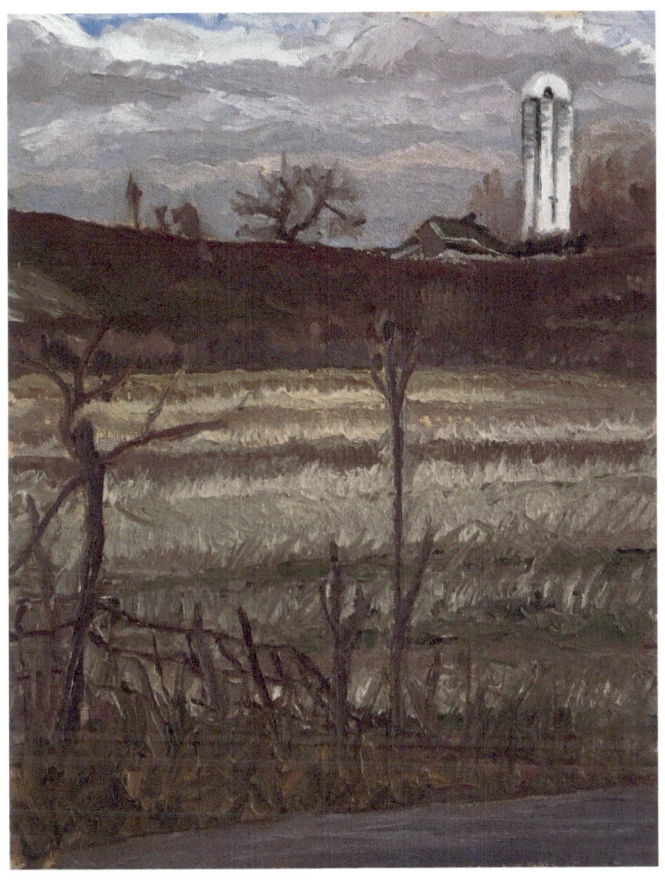

Look closely at the painting above; first notice the clouds in the foreground and then the clouds in the background. The shadows underneath the clouds are very warm in the foreground and cool in the background.

Highlights in clouds work in the opposite manner. Highlights in the clouds nearest the viewer are cooler and lighter in value, while the highlights in the clouds far away from the viewer are warmer and slightly darker in value.

Chapter 5 Step 5 - How to Paint the Background

How to Paint the Background

Now that the sky is painted, we can now start on the background. The more I paint, the more it becomes apparent that the sky sets the entire "KEY" for the rest of the painting. Whatever the sky's color that sky color will be all-pervasive throughout the entire scene.

There is a lot of distance between the viewer and the background. As such, the distant background has a lot of the sky color "KEY" mixed in. Let us consider an example.

There is a distant tree line or hill in a scene. Simply take the sky color that was created for the area of the sky closest to the horizon line. Next, take the tree green color and add a heap of that sky color to it. The result may need adjusted a bit with the addition of cobalt blue and/or titanium white to capture the atmospheric feeling of the day. This should help the aspiring landscape artist get near the tricky color of that distant tree line or hill.

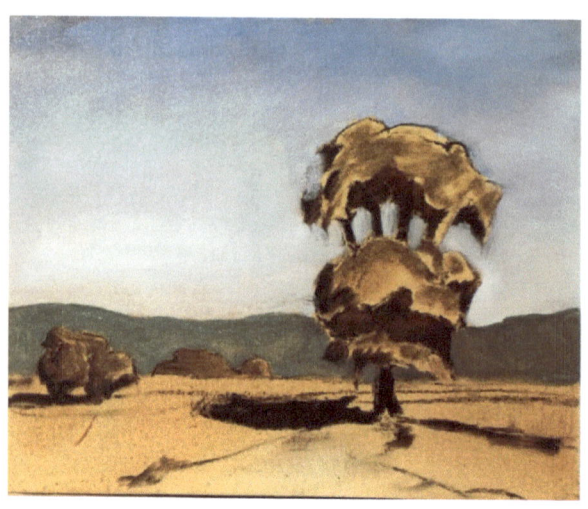

The same holds true for whatever object is in the background. Simply take whatever color the object would be, if one were to be within 10 meters of that object. Consider a distant building. If the building is red, take the red color and add the sky color mixture nearest the horizon to it. Adding the sky color to the objects real color, the artist lightens the value and makes the barn part of the scenes color "KEY." Using this technique creates atmosphere and unity in a Landscape painting.

The last point that needs to be taken into consideration in landscape painting is that the paint in the background should be kept thin. The sky is painted thinly so as not to create something garish. The sky is always somewhat flat and the distant background should be painted flat for the same reason. Painting with thick paint adds too much variation and adds unnecessary competition for the foreground. Distant objects have less detail and have a more uniform color plane. Paint the background flat.

Chapter 6 Step 6 - How to Paint Trees

How to Paint Trees

If the landscape painter lives where there are lots of trees, this chapter will come in handy. If the landscape artist lives in an area that has few trees, it will still be beneficial because most vegetation can be handled in the same manner.

When drawing a tree with charcoal, it is necessary to draw the tree proportionally to the rest of its environment. In other words, be honest and draw the tree to its proper height in relation to the other objects in the composition. It helps to begin drawing the trunks and limbs with charcoal even if they cannot be seen on account of the dense foliage of summer.

The next step is to place the breaks in the foliage in the correct places. It is very easy to become lost in tree foliage. For that reason, create an anchor point on a certain place of the tree. I like to personally use the area where the trunk disappears into the leaves. I say things to myself like: "I can see the sky in this particular break in the foliage and it is at "two o'clock" from the tree trunk. The next break is on the same angle and is approximately one length of charcoal from the last break in the foliage."

Once the tree is drawn in using charcoal and painted with raw sienna, the next step would be to take the tree color green and add some burnt sienna and alizarin crimson and make a pile of paint that closely resembles the darkest shadows underneath the foliage. Take the tree green again and add in yellow ochre, sap green and titanium white in order to create the areas of highlights on top of the foliage.

Now we have three colors for our tree: a dark value tree green, a middle value tree green, and a light value tree green.

Painting trees in accordance with a dark, middle, and light value work well. Take the darkest value tree green and paint in the clusters of foliage. Next apply the middle value tree green. The last step is to take the highest value tree green and paint in the highlights. With any luck and a use of restraint the tree will maintain its structure.

Painting the tree trunk and its limbs is simple. Take a heap of cobalt blue and a heap of burnt sienna. Add to this mixture a heap of titanium white. This recipe makes an excellent gray color that can be used for a tree's trunk, limbs and branches. This mixture can be adjusted to look more brown by adding more burnt sienna or more blue by adding more cobalt blue.

It helps to take a small hog bristle brush and paint in the tree limbs or branches by holding the paintbrush vertically. In other words, hold the brush with its flat sides vertical and pull the paint in one deft stroke from the base of the tree up through the sky. Pulling the paint from the ground up will create dense color near the bottom. As the brush is pulled through the sky color, more paint from the sky will mix with the tree trunk color and cause the branches to become lost into the light of the sky.

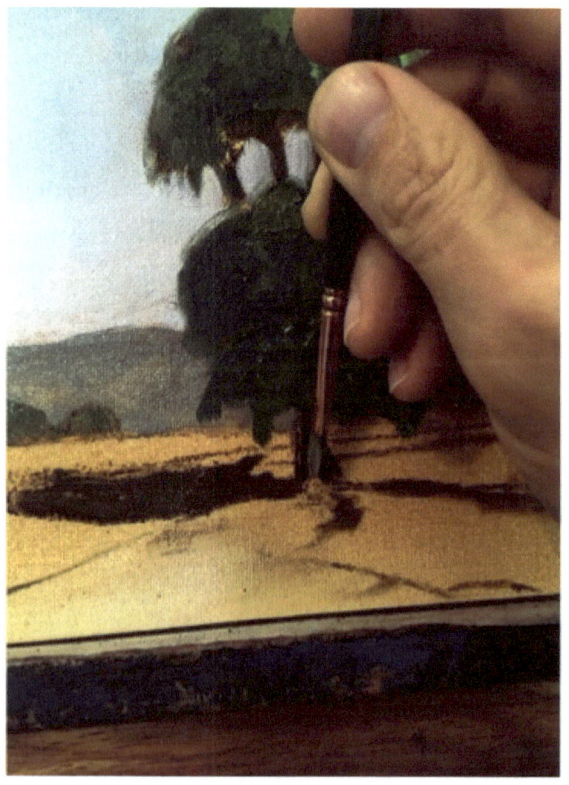

Chapter 7 Step 7 - How to Paint the Foreground

How to Paint the Foreground

The foreground is great fun to paint. Let us suppose the scene is a simple grassy field that the landscape artist would like to paint. The meadow green color is a great place to start. This starting color can be adjusted for any variation in the color of foliage upon the ground.

In the foreground the landscape artist can heap the paint on in order to create texture and added interest. The landscape artist can apply the paint with whatever method they see fit. There is a trick to paint a ground covering with a myriad of leaves, twigs, and grasses.

Simply take the brush and use an up and down motion that goes against the fibers of the brush. This makes the bristles fold over themselves and spring back. This motion creates thousands of switches of grass or at least an effect akin to that thatched illusion.

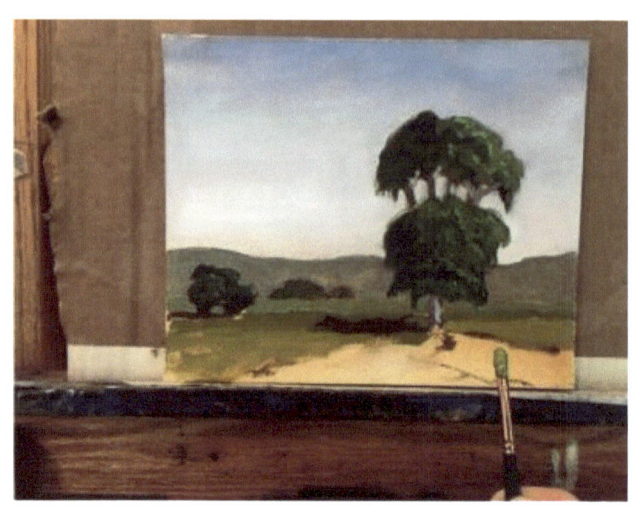

Painting thickly in the foreground can be over done. It is good practice to have a plan and to follow the original charcoal drawing because thick paint can quickly turn into a thick mess. Use restraint through the whole painting by painting the sky and distant objects using thin paint but in the foreground go hog wild with thick paint. It can be so much fun to heap the paint on at this stage and really create excitement and illusion of depth.

Between each stroke, go back onto the palette and pick up some new color. Adding new color to the brush between strokes adds variation but always remember to follow what nature has created in order to experience unity.

It makes sense when painting the earth to use earth tones and colors. These colors are: yellow ochre, raw sienna, burnt sienna, sap green, viridian and plenty of titanium white. Every so often it will become necessary to use colors like: cadmium yellow, cadmium orange and alizarin crimson to really set something off, but if the artist sticks to the earth tones when painting the earth, they will not go astray.

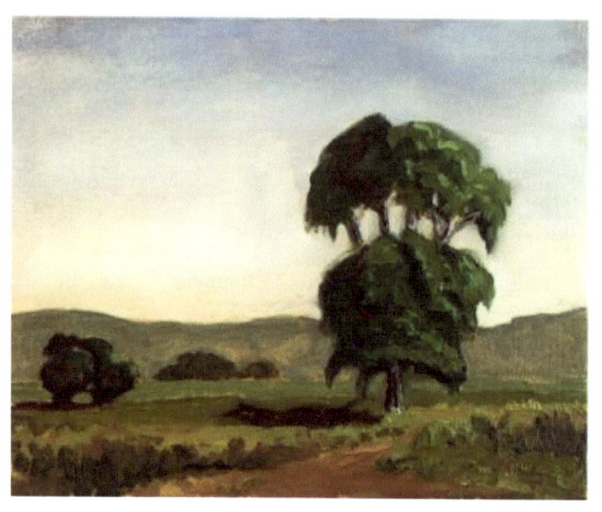

Chapter 8 A Quick Exercise and Conclusion

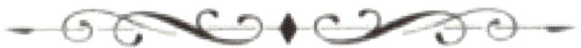

A Quick Exercise and Conclusion

A Quick Exercise

Copy this simple drawing using charcoal onto a raw sienna tinted 8" x 10" canvas board. Use the color recipes previously mentioned and paint away. It is a good idea to experiment with new techniques and colors before venturing out into the field.

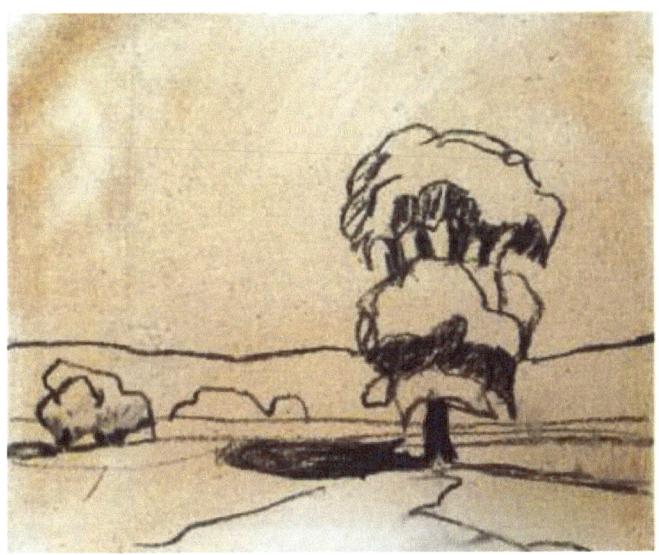

Conclusion

This color palette was created for my location. Depending on where the artist paints, the tree green color and the meadow green color may not match the area. However, the sky blue color when painted upon a raw sienna tinted canvas, will be representative of any clear blue sky.

It was my hope that writing this book has given the reader an excellent starting point. I know when I first started Landscape Painting my biggest desire was to paint that bright blue sky. It took time, a lot of reading, and experimentation to finally figure it out.

Every geographical location has its peculiarities and distinct weather patterns. Figuring out a palette is what lends intrigue to the whole operation of landscape painting. Perhaps these color recipes will fit your area. With continued practice the palette of colors suggested will make natures glory attainable. Start with a solid system and work within that system to find creativity and variation.

My last piece of advice is to use the same set up and to use the same color palette for at least a season or two. Keeping the same routine and painting with the same palette of colors will build fluency. Before one realizes it, they will be able to mix any color and dash in an entire scene in the blink of an eye.

Nature's myriad of color continues to inspire me everyday. With any luck, my techniques, palette and simple color recipes will lend a helping hand. I like to paint outdoors in the changing weather because that is where the magic and inspiration happens. Over six hundred years ago the Italian author and poet, Dante Alighieri, said "Nature is the Art of God." I wish you luck in finding God.

Please rate and write a review of this book online.

Acknowledgements

I would like to acknowledge all my art teachers I have had in the past. Especially Mr. Gary Erbaugh who was my Art teacher at Preble Shawnee High School. It was his measured instruction and understanding that has kept me on the creative path. Thank You Mr. Erbaugh.

So you made it through this little book? I am very glad that you did. Hopefully the instruction given will be useful. If you have particular questions, please find me online for additional resources. I look forward to seeing what will be created from this creation.

All of my artwork is available for sale online as originals or as prints, along with painting tutorials, recommended products, and more.

My Website: http://www.artworkbyjj.com/

Facebook:
https://www.facebook.com/ARTWORKBYJEREMIAHJOLLIFF

Blog: https://jjolliffblog.wordpress.com/

Twitter: https://twitter.com/jeremiahjollif

Youtube:
https://www.youtube.com/channel/UCsauBxqWjjow6bCKl7DgRHA

LinkedIn: https://www.linkedin.com/in/jeremiahjolliff

Instagram: https://instagram.com/jeremiah_jolliff/

Pinterest: https://www.pinterest.com/jeremiahjolliff/

Further Reading and Bibliography

Carlson's Guide to Landscape Painting
By John F. Carlson
(C)1929

> This is the definitive guide to Landscape
> Painting that the serious painter should already
> have in their collection. If they do not have it,
> then they should go buy it immediately.

Hamlet's Mill, An Essay on Myth and the Frame of Time
By Giorgio de Santillana and Hertha von Dechend
(C)1969

> This is a great book that will illuminate the
> mind to the natural events that gave birth to
> this era of increased productivity.

Landscape Painting
By Asher B. Durand and Birge Harrison
(C)2013

> A collection of Letters on Landscape Painting
> from Asher B. Durand with an original
> copyright of 1855 and the second part of the
> book is a reprint of Birge Harrison's book
> entitled *Landscape Painting*. This book is only for
> the individuals who have been initiated by their
> artistic practice out in nature.

The Practice & Science of Drawing
By Harold Speed
(C)1924

A heavy duty treatise on the craft of drawing and its more esoteric applications. Fortunately this is a mandatory book for the serious artist engaged in real life art making.

Oil Painting Techniques and Materials
By Harold Speed
(C)1924

This is the unofficial follow up and sequel to the aforementioned book by the same author.

The Practice of Oil Painting and Drawing
By Solomon Joseph Solomon
(C)1911

Solomon Joseph Solomon's tour de force; before the modern artist and charlatans ransacked the philosophical house of painting, S.J.S. hid the jewels away in this work in the hopes that one day more illuminated benefactors would recover the craft of painting.